11/12/14

When I Grow Up

I CAN BE THE
PRESIDENT

By Alex Appleby

Gareth Stevens
PUBLISHING

Please visit our website, www.garethstevens.com. For a free color catalog of all our high-quality books, call toll free 1-800-542-2595 or fax 1-877-542-2596.

Library of Congress Cataloging-in-Publication Data

Appleby, Alex.
I can be the president / by Alex Appleby.
p. cm. — (When I grow up)
Includes index.
ISBN 978-1-4824-1031-0 (pbk.)
ISBN 978-1-4824-1032-7 (6-pack)
ISBN 978-1-4824-1030-3 (library binding)
1. Presidents — United States — Juvenile literature. I. Appleby, Alex. II. Title.
JK517.A66 2015
352.23—d23

First Edition

Published in 2015 by
Gareth Stevens Publishing
111 East 14th Street, Suite 349
New York, NY 10003

Copyright © 2015 Gareth Stevens Publishing

Editor: Ryan Nagelhout
Designer: Sarah Liddell

Photo credits: Cover, p. 1 (girl) © iStockphoto.com/pkline; cover, p. 1 (White House) spirit of america/Shutterstock.com; p. 5 S-F/Shutterstock.com; pp. 7, 24 (White House) Vacclav/Shutterstock.com; p. 9 Alex Wong/Staff/Getty Images News/Getty Images; p. 11 Barry Winiker/Photolibrary/Getty Images; p. 13 Joseph H. Bailey/National Geographic/Getty Images; p. 15 Eric Thayer/Stringer/Getty Images News/Getty Images; p. 17 Peter Macdiarmid/Staff/Getty Images News/Getty Images; p. 19 Win McNamee/Staff/Getty Images News/Getty Images; p. 21 JEWEL SAMAD/Staff/AFP/Getty Images; pp. 23, 24 (plane) EPG_EuroPhotoGraphics/Shutterstock.com.

Printed in the United States of America

CPSIA compliance information: Batch #CS15GS: For further information contact Gareth Stevens, New York, New York at 1-800-542-2595.

Contents

I want to be president.

4

5

Presidents live
in a big house.
It is called
the White House.

It has many rooms.

I love the Blue Room!

It also has
a large garden.

13

Presidents meet
many people.

Some are important leaders.

Others are big stars!

Presidents work
in a big office.
This is the Oval Office.

21

They have
their own plane!
It is called
Air Force One.

23

Words to Know

plane

White House

Index